21st
Century
Skills Library

GLOBAL PERSPECTIVES

WATERSHED CONSERVATION

Pam Rosenberg

Cherry Lake Publishing
Ann Arbor, Michigan

Published in the United States of America by Cherry Lake Publishing
Ann Arbor, Michigan
www.cherrylakepublishing.com

Content Adviser: Dr. Robin A. Matthews, Director of the Institute for Watershed Studies, Western Washington University, Bellingham, Washington

Photo Credits: Cover and page 1, © iStockphoto.com/winhorse; page 4, © David Kamm/Alamy; page 6, © Diadem Images/Alamy; page 8, © Friedrich Stark/Alamy; page 9, © Neil Cooper/Alamy; page 10, © J. Schwanke/Alamy; page 13, © Steve Allen Travel Photography/Alamy; page 14, © Images of Africa Photobank/Alamy; page 16, © Bill Bachman/Alamy; page 19, © Julio Etchart/Alamy; page 23, © David Pearson/Alamy; page 24, © Terry Whittaker/Alamy; page 26, © JUPITERIMAGES/Creatas/Alamy

Map by XNR Productions Inc.

Library of Congress Cataloging-in-Publication Data
Rosenberg, Pam.
 Watershed conservation / by Pam Rosenberg.
   p. cm.—(Global perspectives)
 Includes index.
 ISBN-13: 978-1-60279-131-2
 ISBN-10: 1-60279-131-7
 1. Groundwater—Juvenile literature. 2. Watersheds—Juvenile literature.
3. Water supply—Juvenile literature. 4. Water conservation—Juvenile
literature. I. Title. II. Series.
 GB1003.8.R67 2008
 363.6'1—dc22   2007039001

*Cherry Lake Publishing would like to acknowledge the work of
The Partnership for 21st Century Skills.
Please visit* www.21stcenturyskills.org *for more information.*

TABLE OF CONTENTS

THE WATER CRISIS

The Colorado River is more than 1,400 miles (2,253 kilometers) long.

Brad gazed out the window at the Colorado River, thinking about the rafting trip his family had taken last year. He could almost feel the spray of the rushing water as he pictured the beautiful shoreline and canyons. His daydream was interrupted as someone tapped him on the shoulder.

"Excuse me, is this the Colorado Room?" asked a slender, dark-haired girl.

"Yes it is," answered Brad. "Hi, I'm Brad Johnson."

"I'm Ronia Abbas. Where are you from, Brad?" she asked.

"Right here in Moab, Utah. How about you? Where are you from?"

"I'm from Israel," Ronia replied. "How did you get interested in overpopulation?"

"Overpopulation?" Brad looked confused. "I'm here as part of the group studying pollution. You're part of the overpopulation group? Then why have we both been called to this meeting?"

Ronia and Brad were attending a workshop for students called Global Issues, Global Solutions. These student leaders from around the world were hoping to leave the workshop with a lot of ideas about what kids and adults could do to help ensure a better future for our planet.

"Let's sit here," Brad said, pointing to a table near the front of the room. Soon a speaker was at the podium.

"Good afternoon! My name is Marie Mosdal. I work for the U.S. Environmental Protection Agency (EPA), and I'm here to talk to you about the world's water crisis."

"Water crisis? What does that have to do with overpopulation or pollution or any of the other topics the groups are working on?" whispered Ronia.

"I don't know. This is a real mystery!" Brad replied.

✧ ✧ ✧

Life on Earth depends on water. Humans can live for about one month without food but only a few days without water. Much of Earth's surface

Irrigation allows farmers to water crops without depending on rainfall.

is covered with water, but 97 percent of that water is salt water. Only 3 percent of Earth's water is freshwater that can be used for drinking and agriculture. Of that 3 percent, only about one-third is available for human use. The other two-thirds is frozen in icebergs and snow. That means everyone on Earth must share about 1 percent of the planet's freshwater.

People use freshwater for drinking and cooking, to irrigate croplands, for sanitation, and to generate power. But with more than 6 billion people in the world, freshwater supplies are decreasing. In many places, water is already in short supply.

The United Nations declared 2003 the International Year of Freshwater. At that time, it was estimated that 40 percent of the people in the world lived in areas with at least moderate water stress, or periods of time when the demand for water is greater than the supply. By 2025, some experts estimate that about 66 percent, or two-thirds, of the world's population will face water stress.

With demand for freshwater growing more quickly than nature can replenish Earth's supply, watershed conservation is becoming more and more important.

"I just don't understand how there can be a water crisis," said Brad, as the speaker took a break. "All you have to do is turn the faucet on and there is plenty of water."

"That's not true in my home country of Ethiopia," said Amara Fassil, a girl seated at the next table. She was part of the group studying women's rights. "Women in some villages must walk more

The United Nations Children's Fund, known as UNICEF, estimates that there are 1.1 billion people in the world without a source of clean drinking water. Another 2.6 billion do not have good sanitation facilities—toilets and running water for washing hands.

Some people are taking the lead in trying to bring clean, safe water to those in need. Water for People is one group working to help people in developing countries who need access to clean water. Visit www.waterforpeople.org to learn more about how you can help.

Women in Ethiopia pump water. In many places around the world, people must gather a supply of water each day.

than a kilometer each day to fill jugs with water. They are very careful not to waste it!"

"Wow!" said the boy seated next to her. "Where I come from in Germany, we never think about having enough water. It is just there. By the way, I'm Karl Mamsch, and I am part of the group studying poverty."

"Nice to meet you," replied the other three students, as they introduced themselves. The four students were getting to know each other when Ms. Mosdal walked back into the room.

CHAPTER TWO

WHAT IS A WATERSHED?

*Women in Zimbabwe gather water from an unsafe
source. The water is not clean and some women have
been attacked by crocodiles at this location.*

"I've never heard of a watershed before," said Ronia. "I don't think it has anything to do with a shed, like the little building my parents store gardening tools in."

"I don't know what a watershed is either," Amara replied. "But it looks like Ms. Mosdal is ready to start speaking again. Maybe we are about to find out."

Imagine that you are a member of your town's planning committee. Two developers have submitted plans for building homes on 10 acres of land near the river that runs through your town. One builder plans on building 10 homes and using materials that will help keep the watershed healthy. The other builder wants to build 20 homes on the site. They would cost less than the first builder's homes because he has no plans to use environmentally friendly materials.

Some committee members want to choose the builder who will build more homes. They argue that more people in more homes will bring in more tax dollars for your town. Other committee members think the town should do all it can to protect the environment. They want to choose the builder who will build environmentally friendly homes.

Which builder's plan would you vote for? Why?

A watershed is an area of land in which water drains into a specific body of water such as a lake, river, or bay. All of the water that flows over or under the ground in that area ends up in the same body of water. Everyone on Earth lives in a watershed. The activities of the people who live in a particular watershed affect the quality of its water. Human activity can also redirect the flow of water in a watershed.

The boundaries of a watershed are defined by nature, not by people. So a watershed may include many different towns and cities and even different countries. For example, Egypt, Ethiopia, and Sudan are three of the countries that share the Nile River watershed.

The way that humans use the land in the watershed has a great effect on the health of the watershed. The land that immediately

Plants that grow on the banks of rivers and streams help to keep the soil in place and keep pollutants out of the water.

surrounds a body of water, known as the riparian area, is especially important. Riparian zones perform many important functions.

Plants that grow in riparian zones help keep soil in place. This is important so that the soil along the banks of a river or stream doesn't erode, or wear away. The plants also help keep sediment and pollutants out of waterways. Trees and other plants that hang over the water help keep the water at the proper temperature. That is important for the fish and other plants and animals that live in the body of water. Plants also provide food and shelter for many kinds of wildlife.

Healthy riparian zones are also important for flood control. When heavy rains soak a watershed area, the riparian zone provides a place for the runoff water to slow down and soak into the ground before reaching the waterway. This helps keep streams and rivers from quickly overflowing their banks and flooding nearby towns.

"Now I understand what watersheds are," said Karl, looking out the window. "I wonder what watershed we're in right now."

"Well, since that is the Colorado River, my guess is that we're in the Colorado River watershed," said Brad.

"I've got my laptop," said Amara. "Let's look it up!" The others gathered around as she used a search engine to input the words "Colorado River watershed."

"You were right, Brad!" said Ronia, pointing to the computer screen. "Look—this Web site says that the Colorado River watershed drains 242,000 square miles (626,777 square kilometers) in the United States and 2,000 square miles (5,180 sq km) in Mexico. People in seven U.S. states—Arizona, California, Colorado, New Mexico, Nevada, Utah, and Wyoming—and in the Mexican states of Sonora and Baja California share

The Hoover Dam hydroelectric power station provides electricity to millions of people in the southwestern United States.

the water of the Colorado River. And hydroelectric power generated by the river supplies about 30 million people with electricity!"

"But look at this," said Karl. "It says that at certain times of the year, the water levels are so low that the Colorado River doesn't reach the Gulf of California. That doesn't sound good! What can cause something like that?"

CHAPTER THREE

PEOPLE AND WATERSHEDS

The Aswan High Dam on the Nile River was completed in 1970.

"There are a lot of people who use the water from the Colorado River," Brad said. "Maybe they are using too much of it."

"I know that building dams on rivers can have a big effect on the land around that river," said Amara. "In Egypt, the great Aswan High Dam was built to keep the Nile River from overflowing its banks. And the dam has helped save people and land from flooding. It also creates a lot of hydroelectric power. But the floods were actually good for the land. They left behind fertile silt from the river. Without that rich sediment, the farmers in Egypt must now use a lot of fertilizer. Also, the Nile Delta is eroding because the sediment is stopped at the dam and can't reach the delta. As a result, the soil of the delta has higher levels of salt in it. And salty soil is not good for growing most crops."

"It seems like even though you are doing something you think will be good for people, it can have unintended bad effects," said Brad. "How can people know if they are making the right decisions when it comes to watersheds?"

Throughout history, people have settled near bodies of water. Being near a source of clean, fresh water is necessary to stay alive. In modern societies, water isn't just used for drinking, cooking, and growing enough food for one family. It is also used in manufacturing and on large farms that grow crops meant to feed many people.

As people settle near lakes, rivers, and streams, they change the land. This is not always good for the health of the watershed. For example, trees and other plants are often cut down to make room for houses and cropland. But when too many trees and plants are removed, the soil has nothing to anchor it. When it rains, the water running toward the

The effects of erosion can be seen along the banks of a creek in Australia.

watershed's main body of water takes soil with it. The land erodes or wears away. That soil ends up in rivers and streams and often causes problems for the animals that live in the water.

As communities grow, more and more buildings are erected. Shopping centers and office buildings with large, concrete parking lots become part of the landscape. That leaves less soft soil to absorb rainwater. When heavy rains come, the water can't be easily absorbed. It runs off quickly toward the nearest river or stream and may cause flooding.

The storm runoff can cause other problems. Many homeowners use fertilizers to help their lawns and gardens grow. Farmers use fertilizers and pesticides to increase crop yields. When water runs across the land, it picks up these chemicals and deposits them in streams and rivers. The water also picks up soil and debris as it makes its way over the land. The soil and debris end up in streams and rivers, too.

As towns get larger, people look for more and more places to build homes and other buildings. Sometimes dams and levees are built to keep rivers and streams within their main channels and lessen the chance of flooding. Then people feel safe building homes closer to the water's edge. But then even more riparian land is lost. It is estimated that in the United States, 90 percent of wetlands habitat has been lost to human development.

Hoover Dam was built in the 1930s to harness the flow of the Colorado River. It was hailed as a marvel of modern engineering. As the United States expanded to the southwest, people were eager to control the river and use its water to create livable farms and cities in the desert. Millions of people in Nevada, Arizona, and California depend on the river's water and the hydroelectric power it generates.

Today, so many people live in the cities that were built in the desert that the water of the Colorado is no longer enough to fulfill their needs. The wetlands of the river's delta are endangered by the reduced flow of the river's water.

If you could go back in time to the 1930s, would you speak out in favor of building the Hoover Dam or would you oppose it? Why?

Why does the loss of wetlands habitat matter? Healthy wetlands absorb runoff and help filter pollutants, such as fertilizers, out of it before it reaches streams, rivers, and lakes. They are also places for sediment to deposit so it doesn't end up in bodies of water. Wetlands also slow down the flow of runoff water, absorbing it slowly to help prevent rivers and streams from overflowing their banks.

Wetlands provide habitat for a variety of plants and animals. Losing our wetlands means we are also in danger of losing many species of plants and animals.

"Wow, it sounds like people have really made some big mistakes when it comes to watershed conservation!" Karl said. "They didn't think things through."

"I'm not sure I completely agree," Ronia said thoughtfully. "I think people enjoy the benefits of things like hydroelectric power from dams. And building homes and businesses close to supplies of water makes sense. But I wonder what can be done to maintain the quality of modern life and the health of watersheds at the same time."

CHAPTER FOUR

WATER SUPPLIES IN DANGER

A man picks garbage out of the Huangpu River in Shanghai, China.

"I'm not sure what can be done," said Brad, gazing out at the river.

"I was talking to a girl from China who said that the rivers that run through cities in her country are dirty and full of pollution. There is much industrial waste dumped in them each day," said Karl.

"But don't forget that in my country, women often walk more than a kilometer to fetch water for their families' needs," said Amara. "These people would welcome development that would bring water to their villages—maybe even if it meant that the watershed would be disturbed.

They are more concerned with having clean water and keeping their children healthy than whether plants and animals might die!"

"There must be something that can be done to balance the needs of everyone," said Ronia.

Water pollution can be divided into two main categories: point source pollution and nonpoint source pollution.

Point source pollution is pollution that comes from a single identifiable source. One example of this kind of pollution is a factory that dumps waste into a lake or river. Another example would be a municipal waste plant that processes sewage that comes from the homes of a city's residents.

Nonpoint sources of pollution are harder to identify. Nonpoint pollution enters waterways in the runoff that flows over the watershed's land and picks up things like sediment, fertilizers, and other pollutants. In less-developed countries without indoor plumbing, runoff may even contain human waste from toilets that are nothing more than holes dug in the ground. By the time the pollutants reach the water, there is no way to identify where a particular pollutant came from.

The Clean Water Act has helped clean up point source pollution in the United States. This act made it illegal for anyone to dump pollutants from a point source into navigable waters. It also gave the Environmental Protection Agency (EPA) the authority to set standards for water quality and helped fund the building of wastewater treatment plants.

Since the passage of this act in 1972, progress has been made. But there is more work to be done. Nearly half of U.S. waters are still not clean enough for safe fishing and swimming. Many industrial plants and municipal wastewater plants are not following the standards set by the EPA. The EPA reports that one-quarter of the nation's largest industrial plants are in serious violation of the Clean Water Act. In addition, it is much harder to clean up nonpoint source pollution. This type of pollution can come from just about anywhere. It may even come from outside the watershed area as pollutants in the air. Chemicals released from industry join with moisture in the air and make their way to the ground in the form of acid rain.

21st Century Content

Governments must try to balance the needs of businesses and economic growth with keeping waterways clean. This is why environmental regulations don't say that no waste can be dumped into lakes and rivers. Instead, scientists and lawmakers work together to come up with standards for how much of each type of pollutant can be dumped.

But people don't always agree on what safe limits are. In 2007, the corporation known as British Petroleum (BP) made plans to dump more ammonia and other waste into Lake Michigan from one of its facilities in Indiana. Citizens and lawmakers in communities along the shoreline organized to protest BP's plan. As a result, BP backed down. In this case, environmental concerns won out over economic development.

The Danube River is the second-longest river in Europe. It is 1,784 miles (2,871 km) long and flows through 10 countries. Several other countries are part of its drainage basin, or watershed. As part of its Trans-European Transport Networks plan, the European Union wants to increase shipping on the Danube. Member nations must decide if this will be done by making boats to fit the river or by altering the channel of the river to fit larger boats. The decision will have a great impact on the future of the river. It will take collaboration and comprise to come up with a plan that is acceptable to all of the nations in the watershed.

The problem of water pollution is even more complicated because water is always moving. And many bodies of water flow through more than one country. The Great Lakes, for example, are shared by the United States and Canada. Even if Canadians released no pollutants into the lakes, they could still have a pollution problem because of wastes dumped into the lakes by U.S. factories and cities.

In China, industries are developing at a rapid pace. Many people in China are able to live more comfortably because of the jobs that these industries provide. But one of the negative side effects of this economic activity is that much pollution is being dumped in China's rivers. Though most of the pollutants come from the large urban areas that contain many factories, people in smaller towns downstream are also affected because the water is dirty when it reaches them.

"I never really thought about how my actions can affect other people when it comes to keeping my watershed clean," said Brad.

"I know what you mean," Amara replied. "I never stopped to think about how each small act of pollution can add up and cause problems for other people— even people far away."

"We need to think about what we can do to help preserve our watersheds and keep our water clean," agreed Ronia. "Now that I know how little of the world's water is good for drinking and agriculture, I know how important it is to manage this precious resource!"

Dead fish float in a stream polluted with chemical waste. People, plants, and animals can all be harmed when water is polluted.

"But how do we know what the right actions are?" asked Karl. "Do people have to choose between economic development and clean water? Or is it possible to have both?"

CHAPTER FIVE

WORKING TOGETHER TO CONSERVE

Students help test the quality of the water in a stream in Vietnam.

"So, as you can see," concluded Ms. Mosdal, "managing our world's watersheds must be a priority in the 21st century."

"Now I see what watershed management has to do with pollution, overpopulation, and lots of other topics!" Ronia said. "It is going to take the efforts and knowledge of people in many different fields to make sure we have enough water and that all of the world's people have access to it."

"You're right," replied Brad. "And we're all going to have to do our part to keep our own local watersheds clean and healthy."

According to the World Wildlife Fund, about 40 percent of the world's people live in watersheds that are under stress or endangered in some way. What are the consequences? If watersheds aren't managed properly, people may become sick, plants and animals (including humans) may die, and communities will not grow and prosper.

What can be done? Community leaders need to have development plans. When people want to build homes or businesses want to build offices and factories, everyone involved needs to make sure that the building projects won't hurt the watershed.

Wherever possible, riparian zones should be preserved when new development is planned. Environmental groups and other concerned citizens should be encouraged to restore lost wetlands habitat.

21st Century Content

The Coca-Cola Company has teamed up with the World Wildlife Fund to work on watershed conservation projects around the world. The two organizations will work to conserve 7 watersheds in more than 20 countries on 4 continents. Why do you think The Coca-Cola Company chose watershed conservation as an environmental project to invest in? Hint: What is the main ingredient in most of Coca-Cola's products?

Turning off the water while you brush your teeth is just one way to save water.

Businesses and cities have to manage wastes properly. The government has set limits on what can be dumped in the nation's waterways. Leaders need to make sure that they operate within these limits.

"So many of the things that need to be done are up to business and community leaders," Karl observed. "I'm not sure what I can do to help."

"There are many things we can do as individuals," Amara responded. "We just need to make up our minds to do them!"

"I have some ideas," said Ronia. "From now on, when I brush my teeth, I'm going to turn the water off while I'm brushing. I'm also going to take quick showers instead of baths."

"I'm going to talk to my parents about not using so much water and fertilizer on our lawn to keep it looking perfect," said Brad. "And I'm going to go to the library and get some books about gardening with native plants. I remember learning that they require a lot less watering and chemicals because they are suited for the climate and soil in your own area."

"Let's make a list of all the things we can think of," suggested Amara. "Call out your ideas, and I'll type them on my laptop!"

"How about using bath water to water plants?"

"Only run the dishwasher and washing machine when you have a full load!"

"Fix dripping faucets."

"Hold on!" laughed Amara. "I can't type that fast. We've got a lot of ideas. Now that we know how important watersheds are, keeping them safe just seems like common sense."

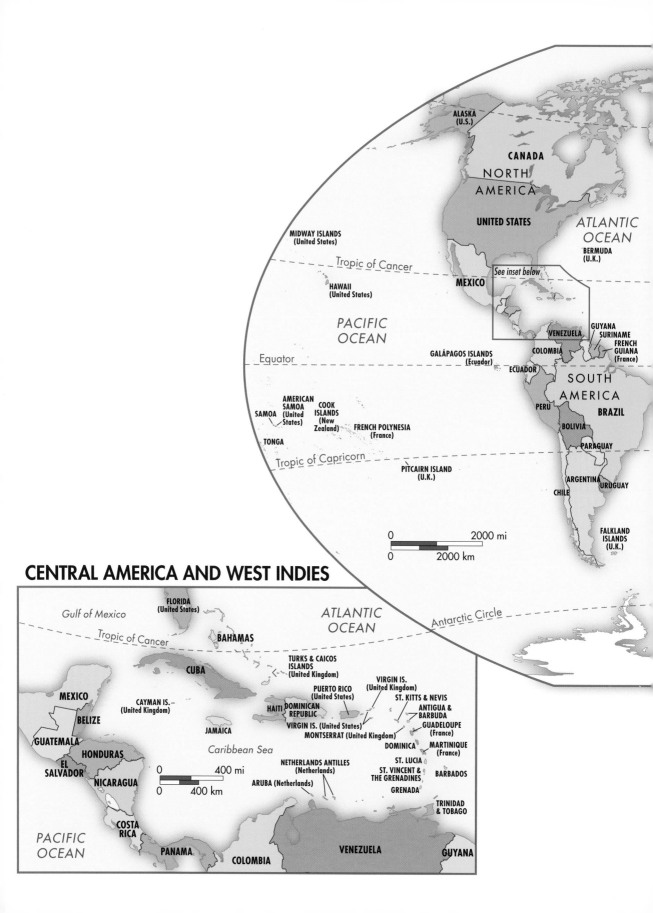

ALASKA
(U.S.)

CANADA

NORTH
AMERICA

UNITED STATES

ATLANTIC
OCEAN

MIDWAY ISLANDS
(United States)

BERMUDA
(U.K.)

Tropic of Cancer

MEXICO

HAWAII
(United States)

See inset below

PACIFIC
OCEAN

GUYANA
SURINAME
VENEZUELA
FRENCH
GUIANA
(France)

COLOMBIA

GALÁPAGOS ISLANDS
(Ecuador)

ECUADOR

Equator

SOUTH
AMERICA

PERU
BRAZIL

AMERICAN
SAMOA
(United
States)

COOK
ISLANDS
(New
Zealand)

SAMOA

BOLIVIA

FRENCH POLYNESIA
(France)

PARAGUAY

TONGA

Tropic of Capricorn

ARGENTINA
URUGUAY

PITCAIRN ISLAND
(U.K.)

CHILE

0   2000 mi

0   2000 km

FALKLAND
ISLANDS
(U.K.)

CENTRAL AMERICA AND WEST INDIES

FLORIDA
(United States)

ATLANTIC
OCEAN

Gulf of Mexico

Antarctic Circle

Tropic of Cancer

BAHAMAS

TURKS & CAICOS
ISLANDS
(United Kingdom)

CUBA

MEXICO

CAYMAN IS.
(United Kingdom)

VIRGIN IS.
(United Kingdom)

PUERTO RICO
(United States)

ST. KITTS & NEVIS

BELIZE

HAITI
DOMINICAN
REPUBLIC

ANTIGUA &
BARBUDA

GUADELOUPE
(France)

GUATEMALA

JAMAICA

VIRGIN IS. (United States)
MONTSERRAT (United Kingdom)

MARTINIQUE
(France)

HONDURAS

Caribbean Sea

DOMINICA

EL
SALVADOR

ST. LUCIA

NICARAGUA

NETHERLANDS ANTILLES
(Netherlands)

ST. VINCENT &
THE GRENADINES

BARBADOS

0   400 mi

0   400 km

ARUBA (Netherlands)

GRENADA

COSTA
RICA

TRINIDAD
& TOBAGO

PACIFIC
OCEAN

PANAMA

COLOMBIA

VENEZUELA

GUYANA

ARCTIC OCEAN

GREENLAND
(Denmark)

SVALBARD
(Norway)

Arctic Circle

ICELAND

RUSSIA

See inset below

ASIA

EUROPE

KAZAKHSTAN

MONGOLIA

GEORGIA

UZBEKISTAN

KYRGYZSTAN

NORTH
KOREA

JAPAN

AZORES
(Portugal)

ARMENIA
TURKEY

TURKMENISTAN

TAJIKISTAN

SOUTH
KOREA

PACIFIC
OCEAN

CANARY
ISLANDS
(Spain)

TUNISIA

SYRIA

LEBANON

AZERBAIJAN

IRAN

AFGHANISTAN

CHINA

MOROCCO

IRAQ

KUWAIT

BAHRAIN

PAKISTAN

BHUTAN

NEPAL

TAIWAN

Tropic of Cancer

ALGERIA

LIBYA

ISRAEL

EGYPT

JORDAN

QATAR

UNITED
ARAB
EMIRATES

BANGLADESH

INDIA

LAOS

WAKE
ISLAND
(United States)

WESTERN
SAHARA
(Morocco)

SAUDI
ARABIA

OMAN

MYANMAR
(BURMA)

THAILAND

VIETNAM

NORTHERN
MARIANA ISLANDS
(United States)

GUAM
(United States)

MARSHALL
ISLANDS

CAPE
VERDE

MAURITANIA

MALI

NIGER

CHAD

SUDAN

ERITREA

YEMEN

SENEGAL

BURKINA
FASO

BENIN

AFRICA

DJIBOUTI

SRI
LANKA

PHILIPPINES

PALAU

FEDERATED STATES
OF MICRONESIA

GAMB.

GUINEA

GHANA

NIGERIA

CENTRAL
AFRICAN
REP.

ETHIOPIA

SOMALIA

CAMBODIA

BRUNEI

MALAYSIA

KIRIBATI

GUINEA-
BISSAU

CAMEROON

MALDIVES

Equator

SIERRA
LEONE

LIBERIA

CÔTE
D'IVOIRE

TOGO

RWANDA

UGANDA

KENYA

NAURU

SAO TOME AND
PRINCIPE

EQUATORIAL
GUINEA

GABON

DEM. REP.
OF THE
CONGO

BURUNDI

TANZANIA

INDONESIA

EAST
TIMOR

PAPUA
NEW
GUINEA

SOLOMON
ISLANDS

CONGO

SEYCHELLES

TUVALU

ATLANTIC
OCEAN

ANGOLA

ZAMBIA

MALAWI

COMOROS

INDIAN
OCEAN

NAMIBIA

ZIMBABWE

BOTSWANA

MADAGASCAR

MAURITIUS

VANUATU

FIJI
ISLANDS

N

W   E

S

MOZAMBIQUE

SWAZILAND

SOUTH
AFRICA

LESOTHO

RÉUNION
(France)

Tropic of Capricorn

AUSTRALIA

AUSTRALIA

NEW
CALEDONIA
(France)

FRENCH SOUTHERN &
ANTARCTIC LANDS
(France)

NEW
ZEALAND

SOUTH GEORGIA &
SOUTH SANDWICH
ISLANDS (U.K.)

Antarctic Circle

ANTARCTICA

EUROPE

NORWAY

SWEDEN

FINLAND

RUSSIA

North
Sea

DENMARK

ESTONIA

Baltic Sea

LATVIA

IRELAND

UNITED
KINGDOM

LITHUANIA

RUSSIA

BELARUS

0   400 mi

0   400 km

NETH.

BELG.

GERMANY

POLAND

LUX.

CZECH
REPUBLIC

UKRAINE

ATLANTIC
OCEAN

LIECH.

SLOVAKIA

FRANCE

SWITZ.

AUSTRIA

HUNGARY

MOLDOVA

SLOVENIA

ROMANIA

MONACO

CROATIA

SAN MARINO

BOS. &
HERZ.

SERBIA

Black Sea

GEORGIA

PORTUGAL

ANDORRA

SPAIN

ITALY

MONT.

MACEDONIA

BULGARIA

ALBANIA

TURKEY

GIBRALTAR (U.K.)

GREECE

MOROCCO

ALGERIA

TUNISIA

MALTA

Mediterranean Sea

CYPRUS

SYRIA

LEBANON

Glossary

agriculture (AG-ruh-kul-chur) the practice of farming, growing crops and raising livestock

channels (CHAN-uhlz) narrow stretches of water between two areas of land

delta (DEL-tuh) an area of land shaped like a triangle where a river deposits mud, sand, or pebbles as it enters the sea

European Union (yu-ruh-PEE-uhn YOON-yuhn) an established committee of European countries that work to solve issues affecting Europe

hydroelectric (hye-droh-ih-LEK-trik) having to do with the production of electricity using water power to turn a generator

pollutants (puh-LOOT-uhntz) anything that contaminates or pollutes something else

riparian (rih-PAR-ee-uhn) related to living or located on the banks of a river

sanitation (san-uh-TAY-shuhn) the process of cleaning the water supply and disposing of sewage

sediment (SED-uh-muhnt) rocks, sand, or dirt that has been carried to a place by water

silt (SILT) fine particles of soil that are carried along by flowing water and eventually settle to the bottom of a body of a river or lake

water stress (WAH-tur STRESS) periods of time when the demand for water is greater than the supply watershed conservation (waH-tur-she kon-sur-VAY-shuhn) protection of the land that drains into rivers and other bodies of water

wetlands (WET-landz) areas of land where there is much moisture in the soil

FOR MORE INFORMATION

Books

Bowden, Rob. *Earth's Water Crisis*. Milwaukee, WI: World Almanac Library, 2007.

Royston, Angela. *The Life and Times of a Drop of Water*. Chicago: Raintree, 2006.

Somervill, Barbara A. *Rivers, Streams, Lakes, and Ponds*. Mankato, MN: Tradition Books, 2004.

Web Sites

Alliance for Watershed Action and Riparian Easements: Kids
www.watershed.cboss.com/kids.htm
Ideas about how to save water along with links to information on the water cycle, a water puzzle, and a quiz to test your knowledge

United States Environmental Protection Agency—Environmental Kids Club
www.epa.gov/kids/water.htm
Information and activities about the importance of keeping water clean

Water for People
www.waterforpeople.org
Learn more about how Water for People brings access to fresh water and sanitation to people around the world

Water Use It Wisely—100 Water-Saving Tips
www.wateruseitwisely.com/100ways
Click on your state to find 100 things you can do to save water

INDEX

ABOUT THE AUTHOR

Pam Rosenberg has written more than 30 books for young people. A former teacher and corporate trainer, she currently works full time as a writer and editor. She lives in Arlington Heights, Illinois.